Black Sheep

curious directive

***methuen* | drama**
LONDON • NEW YORK • OXFORD • NEW DELHI • SYDNEY

METHUEN DRAMA

Bloomsbury Publishing Plc, 50 Bedford Square, London, WC1B 3DP, UK
Bloomsbury Publishing Inc, 1359 Broadway, New York, NY 10018, USA
Bloomsbury Publishing Ireland, 29 Earlsfort Terrace, Dublin 2, D02 AY28, Ireland

BLOOMSBURY, METHUEN DRAMA and the
Methuen Drama logo are trademarks of Bloomsbury Publishing Plc

First published in Great Britain 2025

Copyright © curious directive, 2025

curious directive have asserted their right under the Copyright, Designs
and Patents Act, 1988, to be identified as Author of this work.

Cover image by Katherine Mager

All rights reserved. No part of this publication may be: i) reproduced or transmitted in
any form, electronic or mechanical, including photocopying, recording or by means of
any information storage or retrieval system without prior permission in writing from
the publishers; or ii) used or reproduced in any way for the training, development or
operation of artificial intelligence (AI) technologies, including generative AI technologies.
The rights holders expressly reserve this publication from the text and data mining
exception as per Article 4(3) of the Digital Single Market Directive (EU) 2019/790.

Bloomsbury Publishing Plc does not have any control over, or responsibility for,
any third-party websites referred to or in this book. All internet addresses given in this
book were correct at the time of going to press. The author and publisher regret
any inconvenience caused if addresses have changed or sites have ceased
to exist, but can accept no responsibility for any such changes.

No rights in incidental music or songs contained in the work are hereby granted
and performance rights for any performance/presentation whatsoever
must be obtained from the respective copyright owners.

All rights whatsoever in this play are strictly reserved and application for performance
etc. should be made before rehearsals begin to the author via Bloomsbury Publishing,
performance.permissions@bloomsbury.com. No performance may be given
unless a licence has been obtained.

A catalogue record for this book is available from the British Library.

A catalog record for this book is available from the Library of Congress.

ISBN: PB: 978-1-3506-1316-4
       ePDF: 978-1-3506-1317-1
       eBook: 978-1-3506-1318-8

Series: Modern Plays

Typeset by Westchester Publishing Services
Printed and bound in Great Britain

For product safety related questions contact productsafety@bloomsbury.com.

To find out more about our authors and books visit
www.bloomsbury.com and sign up for our newsletters.

BLACK SHEEP

by curious directive

Norfolk, circa 1985-1995.
Picking strawberries in Sharrington. Waiting for the school bus in Langham. Gillie-crabbing on the quay in Blakeney. Watching a flooded lane leading to the North Sea in Cley. If you know North Norfolk, perhaps these places, these moments will mean something to you. Growing up rurally is a gift. Not just for someone who, many years later, has become a theatre director and writer. Rural life, especially now, isn't just a different pace – it's a different way of feeling connected. But rural life, and in particular North Norfolk, is changing. There are 3rd homeowners with seagull-cackling RP accents, piercing the serenity of these big skies. But there's a quieter story. The farmers, guardians of the land, are struggling more than any time in recent memory.

National Theatre, London, September 2023.
curious directive, the company I run, has been invited to join the National Theatre Generate Programme - a support system for companies making work which will premiere outside of London. I've gathered a team of actors and creatives, each with a specific connection to rural life, to farming. We discuss character, story, scenography – but also, we think about perspective. We decide that this play will be vociferously from the point of view of farmers. So we gather farmers from Norfolk. We go to see some of them, others come to us. We discuss family, always family. We discuss the climate. We discuss politics, across the spectrum. Types of soil. Arable, livestock – machinery. To stage a response, a homage to the world of farming, a place where food is grown and reared, feels like a big task. I find myself questioning my background, my assumptions, my knowledge. My heritage. Questions are asked in the rehearsal room about farming, and I, somehow, know the answer. Index cards of childhood; Strawberries in Sharrington, the bus in Langham, the quay in Blakeney, the storm in Cley.

Norwich, April 2024.
I'm waiting for the acting company to arrive. I'm sat outside our Studio space in Norwich, which happens to be a church. In the garden, a crocus is appearing through the lawn. The Kerria is about to bloom. The sun is holding me with warmth. This feels like the right time to make a play about Norfolk, about farming. We gather in the Studio and explore how a farming family would, and could, be together every Easter. We play games together. Sub-plots emerge. We don't want to shy away from the brutality of the life of a farmer.

The fathers in the family trees of our characters become important people, even if they aren't on stage. The role of community, of the Christian church in the 21st century. We circle around Chekhov's themes. We begin to work through scenes set in North Norfolk. Straw bales arrive at rehearsals. Their smell filling the air. Lambing gates flank the stage. Their weight, a reality of the physical strength required to rear livestock. Theo Whitworth, my long-time collaborator, provides a heart-breaking violin piece entitled 'Spring'. Healthy topsoil arrives, and we spread it across the floor of the set, made up of a farm kitchen and six chairs. We visit a family leaving their tenant farm and, as such, must get rid of an Aga which has been there for 40 years. We take the Aga apart and use the top and facia on the set. We realise that our design is comprised of 'found' materials. Their provenance, like mycelium, making their way through the story we are building together is palpable Fittingly, a eulogy is written, last minute, as we piece together the final moments of the story. We open the show, which is full of laughter and, at times, not a dry eye in the house. We sense we've captured something accurate, of this special place.

Norwich, October 2025.
We are back together. Exploring the story again, ahead of a UK tour. It's our first time on the road for a long time. The thought of taking this personal story into city contexts, places that perhaps have lost their connection to the land, feels like a necessity. We have lost our connection with the land. Our story is dedicated to farmers past, present and future. To their stoicism. They deserve better. We must try to do better to support them. So, I have one request. Wherever you live, seek out your local market garden/gardener. Consider supporting them. You'll taste the best fruit and vegetables you've ever had. You'll wonder why you've been putting up with the bland food in the supermarket. You'll be supporting locality, encouraging the soil to re-generate and, in turn, you'll much feel better for it. Amen.

Jack Lowe

Jack Lowe, picking strawberries in Sharrington - c.1990

The devising company first gather at the National Theatre Studio - 2023

The devising company visit Patrick Murtimer's farm - September 2023

The devising company visit Branthill Farm, Wells-next-the-Sea - April, 2024

The devising company exploring maps of North Norfolk - April, 2024

Craig Hamilton and Jack Lowe explore the local jokes in the story. - Norwich, 2024

A site visit to Norwich livestock market - April 2024

Much of our time creating the story took place around the kitchen table. Matilda Ziegler, Lewis Mackinnon & Jack Lowe, mid-discussion. - April 2024

The straw arrives in a Luton van outside our creation space - April, 2024

The family, gathered.

Bonnie (Amanda Hadingue) sat at the kitchen table as Elias (Lewis Mackinnon) delivers a sermon.

Darren (Sophie Steer) explores his faith.

The livestock market.

Maggie (Matilda Ziegler) says goodbye to the farm.

Bartlett (Robert Macpherson) clutches a map of North Norfolk.

Petra (Mila Carter) returns to the farm where her parents met.

BLACK SHEEP *is a curious directive production, supported by the National Theatre Generate Programme.*

devised by curious directive, **conceived by Jack Lowe.**

ORIGINAL CAST

Bonnie Carter / Heather Bagnell / Sandra Martins	**Amanda Hadingue**
Elias Carter / Adrian Loch	**Lewis Mackinnon**
Peter Carter / Bartlett de Toit / Rex Tilbury	**Robert Macpherson**
Maggie Henderson / Rachel de Toit / Julie Wash	**Matilda Ziegler**
Hannah Henderson / Darren Dickson / Sam Wain	**Sophie Steer**
Alina Bondar / Danny Dickson / Petra Carter	**Mila Carter**

CREATIVES

Direction	**Jack Lowe**
Associate Director	**Craig Hamilton**
Design	**Zoë Hurwitz**
Light	**Alex Fernandes**
Sound	**Helen Atkinson**
Composition	**Theo Whitworth**
Video	**Ellie Thompson**
Farmers	**Charles Sayer, Ted & Max Maufe, Patrick Murtimer**
Photography	**Katherine Mager**

ADDITIONAL CREATIVES / TECHNICAL CONTRIBUTIONS

Zoë Aldrich, Maryam Grace, Richard Katz, Patrick Osborne, Kieran Lucas, Pete Malkin & Hamish Mcdougall.

CURIOUS DIRECTIVE (2025)

Artistic Director / CEO	**Jack Lowe**
Producer	**Molly Farley**

www.curiousdirective.com

Black Sheep

Characters

THE FAMILY

THE CARTERS

Bonnie Carter, *mid-60s, farmer, mother to* Peter *and* Elias
Peter Carter, *mid-30s, farmer, son of* Bonnie *and older brother to* Elias
Elias Carter, *early 30s, Church of England priest, son of* Bonnie *and younger brother to* Peter

Aline, *late 20s, PhD student at John Innes Centre, living with the Carters*

THE HENDERSONS

Maggie Henderson, *early 60s, lawyer, sister to* Bonnie
Hannah Henderson, *late 30s, environmental activist, daughter to* Maggie

OTHER CHARACTERS

Heather Bagnell, *mid 60s, farming councillor*
Sandra Martins, *estate agent*
Julie Wash, *mid-60s, Blakeney Housing Association*
Sam Wain, *mid-30s, Blakeney Housing Association*
Rex Tilbury, *mid-30s, National Trust*
Adrian Loch, *mid-30s, National Trust*

Petra Carter, *late 20s, entrepreneur*

THE AIRBNB GUESTS

Rachel de Toit, *early 60s, billionairess, mother to* Bartlett
Bartlett de Toit, *mid-30s, businessmen*

THE NEIGHBOURS

Danny Dickson, *early 30s, fallen live-stock remover*
Darren Dickson, *mid-30s, fallen live-stock remover*

In the text, where used between lines, a forward slash (/) denotes an active silence. Where a forward slash (/) is used mid-dialogue, this can be read as a 'gentle' overlapping of lines. Where an em dash (—) is used, this can be read as a 'hard' interruption, a deliberate cutting off of a thought. In particularly important moments, some text captures the Norfolk dialect. Choices about who has a Norfolk accent, and who does not, is at the discrepancy of the production. It's important to note that the character of Aline, and her origins, is also flexible. It was a specific intention, in the creation of the play, that the farm is housing an academic from lands beyond England. But this academic could come from anywhere in the world and be any gender. Although care should be taken around the character arc of Peter in this choice. Farms have always been places of sanctuary. This production proudly sits within that tradition.

Black Sheep *is set across three acts on the same land. Act One is the present day. Act Two is a year later, and Act Three is in the year 2049. The piece was developed with twelve farmers throughout Norfolk. The majority of the writing came from Jack Lowe, also director of the show, who grew up on a small farm in Norfolk. The intention for the play is to shine a light on the incredible sacrifices farmers undergo day in, day out. At times, the story feels as if it is emerging from the land itself. Crucially, the perspective is very much from the rural characters, with the urban characters (and perspectives) very much taking a back seat. The piece is designed to deliver a love letter to Norfolk, to farming, and to the land itself.*

Act One: EASTER 2025

A farmhouse, Norfolk, Easter. A large pine table with six chairs sits in the middle of a large kitchen. On the table is a pile of soil and two 1:25 toy tractors – one modern, one from the 1950s.

In the kitchen there's an old Aga, a butler's sink, a record player, a photograph of Cley church.

The floor is sage green tiles, with soil furrows running from the audience and into the wall. The kitchen is surrounded on three sides by a 20-centimetre flint wall.

Towards the back of the kitchen there is a stepped straw bale stack, rising up to create a wall of straw. We can see lambing gates and other farming equipment scattered across the straw.

Finally, there is a church pew along the main wall of the kitchen.

On the pew, sat quietly, we can see **Maggie**, **Hannah**, **Alina**, **Peter**, **Bonnie**, *and* **Elias**.

Some church organ music is playing. We're in an Easter service. We see two stained glass windows projected across the straw bale stack.

The music swells and **Peter** *stands. He moves to the farmhouse kitchen table and looks at the soil for a moment.*

Live video captures **Peter**'s *actions from above, which is projected across the straw. This perspective, from above, is a useful motif for use later on in the story. The birds-eye view is fitting for a story about the land, like looking down onto a map.*

Peter *makes a cross in the soil with his hands, as if summoning the rest of the family. One by one* **Maggie**, **Hannah**, **Alina**, **Bonnie** *and* **Elias** *join* **Peter**.

Peter *brings out a map of North Norfolk and unfolds it onto the soil. The family begin to trace the rivers, the roads, tracks and the fields. The family crouch by the table.*

The map is folded back up.

Maggie and Bonnie begin to play with the 1:25 tractors across the soil, the family join.

Once this is established, Elias breaks away, still watching his family, contemplating the significance of family together.

He goes to a microphone to the side of the kitchen, which is used throughout the story, and begins an Easter sermon.

Prologue: in the church

Elias Good morning, everyone. Thank you all for braving it here this morning after that unseasonal storm.

Whilst I remember, this Sunday, we'll be hiding some Easter eggs in the grounds outside – 100 I'm told. So, if anyone fancies a little hunt, there are sugar highs to be found!

Today, Good Friday, marks the beginning of Jesus's journey to the cross. And this morning, we see the first signs of spring, and I'm wondering what that means for you. Is it a newfound energy when rising in the morning? Bulbs bringing new life, new colour or the blossom of a tree by the bus stop.

We hear the sounds of tractors, sheep huddled together.

As many you know, my family are farmers. And so, for me the first sign of spring is in the soil. It's the smell of the soil. The soil coming to life. Spurred on by the sunshine.

We see Alina with a microscope looking at the health of the soil on the kitchen table.

And we're very blessed at St Thomas's to still have many of our original stained-glass windows. And on sunny mornings like this one, I am struck by the magnificent lighting design afforded by the presence of both the glass and the sun.

The family begin to leave the kitchen, with Elias alone with his sermon. The only person who remains in the kitchen is Bonnie, a striking, strong female farming figure.

With the sun shining in through, I was drawn to a very particular stained-glass window. It depicts a flock of sheep in a field, perhaps close to here. There's a farmer in the background, who has stopped to watch. And it reminded me of this from Proverbs.

'Be sure you know the conditions of your flocks, give careful attention to your herds; for riches do not endure forever, and a crown is not secure for all generations'.

A fitting image for our little church, sat above the North Sea, overlooking all our farming brothers and sisters.

The family begin to flood into the kitchen again showing us snapshots of their story.

'The Hay appeareth and the tender grass soweth itself. And herbs of the mountains are gathered. The lambs are for thy clothing and the price of the field. And thou shall have milk enough for thy food, for the food of thy household and the maintenance of thy family'.

Scene One: Maggie (arrives) and Bonnie

It's raining. The kitchen is in a dim light.

Bonnie *is alone, asleep at the kitchen table.*

Maggie *enters the kitchen with her raincoat on. She dries her coat on the Aga and moves the kettle onto the hot plate. She takes in the salt marsh out the window.*

She takes out of her bag a sapling of a Kerria plant – with a yellow firework-esque flower.

She places it gently in front of **Bonnie,** *who wakes.*

Bonnie   Oh, Maggie.

Maggie   Bonnie. Skinny.

Bonnie   I'm trim.

They quietly embrace.

Maggie A specimen. From my Highbury greenhouse. A gift from your North London family.

Bonnie You remembered. I love Kerria. Look at those little flowers. Like fireworks. How was the drive? The A11.

Maggie Filthy. Flash floods slowed us right down.

Bonnie Where's Hannah?

Maggie She's mooching. Stomping around. Re-establishing her roots. Cuppa?

Bonnie I can manage. I can manage.

/

Maggie This Easter time. So good when we get together.

Bonnie And this time no-one's digital. I've had enough of those Zoom boxes.

Maggie This table.

Bonnie We had it cleaned. Used to be covered in your biro doodles.

Maggie You were born on this. I remember it, vividly. They plopped Mum and your placenta right. There.

Bonnie Graphic. Thank you.

Alina *enters.*

Alina You must be Maggie.

Maggie I am!

Alina I've heard so much / about you, all good things.

Bonnie This is Alina. She is probably the cleverest person that's ever stood in this kitchen. She's doing a PhD at the John Innes Centre.

Alina Yes.

Maggie Oh brilliant. On what?

Alina I'm looking at the health of soil on coastal farms at / the moment.

Maggie Oh well this is the place!

Alina Sorry I'm a little late. I need to take the microscope and get to class. I'm doing some teaching – need to sing for my supper!

Bonnie Alina is a demon at Pictionary.

Alina *exits. A moment.*

Maggie Oh, she's a breath of air, isn't she? How did that happen?

Bonnie She's helping in the house too.

Maggie You could do with the help.

Bonnie We get a small grant for hosting. Need every penny we can get at the moment. Have you seen the sign?

Maggie What sign?

Bonnie They've put part of the estate on the market. Since Mr Young's son took over, he's not interested in tenant farmers.

Maggie He can't do that before the / end of your tenancy

Peter *enters.*

Peter As I live and breathe. Aunty Maggie.

Maggie Hello Peter.

Bonnie How are they doing? / There's a package for you that's come, iodine I think.

Peter Just come for the bottles. Is that your car?

Maggie Guilty.

Peter *exits*.

Bonnie Working himself to the bone.

/

Maggie What's the latest from our neighbourly friends the Dicksons?

Bonnie Well. You've seen the shed, cutting straight across the upper field.

Maggie Yes, I saw the shed. It is a monstrosity.

Bonnie They're furious we've struck a deal with the National Trust. Now our sheep are stepping on their cattle grazing apparently.

Maggie Well, the National Trust own the land, they can do whatever they like. Can't you just speak to Edna about it?

Bonnie She's worse than him, and those boys. Christ.

Maggie He must be out soon.

Bonnie Darren?

Maggie Yeah. Blimey.

Bonnie It'll be fine. I've heard he's a changed man.

Elias *enters ready for church, dog collar on.*

Elias Aunty Mags. Hello. You look well. How was your drive?

Maggie Horrible. Look at you. Oh, my lord! (*Referring to the dog collar.*)

Bonnie Look what Maggie brought up for me. (*Referring to the Kerria.*)

Elias I'll be back in a couple of hours.

Bonnie Elias. Will you stop by the chemists for me?

Elias Sure.

Act One: EASTER 2025, Scene Two   11

Elias *exits.*

Bonnie   It's like a merry-go-round in here.

Scene Two: Danny and Darren – Good Friday

We hear the faint sounds of drum and bass, which rises to a huge sound, supported by images of animal carcasses projected across the straw.

Seemingly from nowhere, we see brothers **Danny** *and* **Darren**.

Danny *the younger and* **Darren** *the older. They are in the cab of a Ford Transit van, muddy workwear, woolly hats.* **Danny** *has just collected Darren from HMP Wayland.*

The music soars and then cuts into a series of short scenes.

DARREN IS OUT

Darren, *noisily eating a Big Mac and fries.*

Darren   Oh my god. That's beautiful. 569 days locked up. Feels like I've been fastin'.

Danny   Give us a chip Darren?

Darren   You jokin', had your chance, Danny.

Danny   Chip Darren.

Darren   Woah, woah, woah. Why are you not going up Holt road?

Danny   We're taking the NDR. Need to drop off the heifer first.

The music and sound interrupt, propelling them further forwards in time.

We see **Danny** *and* **Darren** *collecting dead animals and throwing them in the back of the van. This can be done using the straw bales as the carcasses.*

IN THE LAY-BY

They are resting in a lay-by off the main road.

Danny *is asleep.* **Darren** *sucks his finger and very slowly puts it into* **Danny**'s *ear.*

Danny *wakes with a start.*

Danny Fuck off Darren!

The music and sound interrupt, propelling them further forwards in time.

We see **Danny** *and* **Darren** *collecting dead animals and throwing them in the back.*

SING ALONG

Danny *and* **Darren** *are belting 'Living on a Prayer' by Bon Jovi at the top of their lungs.*

Just before the chorus, the music and sound interrupt, propelling them further forwards in time.

We see **Danny** *and* **Darren** *collecting dead animals and throwing them in the back.*

ARRIVING HOME

Darren Brown and Co.? Carters are movin' on are they? Mr Young's finally had enough of Peter's 'diversification'.

Danny Got Airbnb going now in the windmill, haven't they?

Darren Fuck off. Why can't they just farm?

/

Danny Rest of the Carter clan arrived this mornin'.

Darren Oh Right. Oh yeah, Tesla. I'd love to try a go in one of them.

/

Howm sweet home. Aw. Hot bath.

Danny Gotta howse down back first.

Darren You howse down back first.

I'm having a bubble bath and then have a little wander around the graveyard of St Thomas's.

/

Danny Go easy on Mum when you get in. She's fraajul.

/

Darren The boundary dispewt? None of their fuckin' business. We need that shed to store the straw for the cattle. I don't care if it blocks the view to the marshes.

The music and sound interrupt, propelling them out of the van.

We see **Danny** *and* **Darren** *collecting dead animals.*

Scene Three: Rachel and Bartlett

We hear the sound of two RAF tornado jets dogfighting across the marshes, circling the North Sea.

The sound brings **Rachel** *into the scene. She's an American billionairess, dressed in a dark suit, sunglasses and dragging an expensive suitcase.* **Rachel** *is on the phone.*

She's with her son, **Bartlett***, dressed in a black turtleneck with dark glasses and a fanny pack. He surveys the landscape of the North Sea and the farm as* **Rachel** *talks on the phone to* **Alina***.*

Rachel Yes. It's Rachel. *Rachel*. And my son Bartlett. I know we made good time. I hope we're not too early. Who am I speaking to? Alina? Yes — the thing is the driver . . . haha I know pot-holes on your farm track.

That is so kind. (*To Bartlett*) She's coming to get us. Thank you.

Bartlett There is it — 'The Windmill'. On the Airbnb listing, it says it used to be a working mill on the farm. One of only fifteen along the coastal road. And on arrival they will present us with a hamper with bread and jams. Cute.

Rachel Cute. What's for dinner?

Bartlett Moreston Hall is delighted to offer a spring tasting menu. Blah blah blah . . . Huh. They've got a Cromer crab ravioli with a spinach bouillabaisse. We wanted to go to Cromer.

Rachel I know that crabs are scavengers, but they taste so delicious. I don't want to be thinking about anythi — oh will you look the little lambs. So cute. Are they on the menu?

Bartlett Yes. Lamb Three ways.

Rachel I was expecting it to be . . .

Bartlett Shoulder, loin and belly

Rachel . . . Really flat.

Bartlett And these are the Norfolk black Horns.

Rachel Oh little black Horns. (*Imitates them.*)

Bartlett And you know what makes this farm unique, the lamb is fed on the salt marsh.

Rachel Oh there she is . . . Alina. Alinnna!

Scene Four: Bonnie and Elias Easter Saturday, 7.30am

The farm kitchen. It's early, a dreary morning. **Elias** *is listening to St John Passion by Bach.*

Bonnie *enters, sees her son. Fondly watches him.*

Elias How are you getting on?

Bonnie Oh, it's a mudbath out there. There's an oak down in Douglas Meadow. A fuw panels off the brewing barn, some fencing.

Elias I could take a tractor down there later.

Bonnie Yeah.

Elias What are you doing out there anyway? You should be resting.

Bonnie I can't sleep at the minute, so I might as well make myself useful.

Elias *takes* **Bonnie**'s *hands.*

Elias Cold.

Bonnie What time is it?

Elias 7.33.

Bonnie Oof.

Elias How's Peter?

Bonnie Brave face. Lost two ewes on the marsh. One had gone down a gulley, and the other one just wondered off towards the sea. They were both carrying twins so, really, that's six more. 28 in total so far gone.

What are you up to?

Elias Getting ready for the service later.

Bonnie Ah yes.

Elias My third coffee. Holy Saturday. They day where nothing happens. One of life's waiting places.

Bonnie Blimey.

Elias What do you think of this?

Elias *moves to the sermon microphone. It transports* **Bonnie** *and* **Elias** *into the church.* **Elias** *continues.*

'We must not be afraid of the long unspectacular waiting, of which much of life is made up, nor must we be too urgent for the coming of every Easter in our lives, lest we fail to learn from the silence before the first Halleluiah breaks forth'.

Bonnie *applauds.* **Elias** *sits back at the table.*

Bonnie   Ohh. Your Granny, Granny P, loved Holy Week.

Elias   Yeah.

Bonnie   Yes. It was Reverend Hal back then.

Elias   What was he like?

Bonnie   Oh god, terrible! Said whatever came to his head. Improvised his way through it. Couldn't hear anything he said. I think she just liked the flower arrangements and the free jammy dodgers they give out at the end. It was a good gossip session back then too. St Thomas's she went to. Religiously.

Elias   Oh yeah.

Bonnie   Camelias growing around the gate.

Elias   Still there.

/

Elias   My third Easter Saturday this afternoon. What would Granny P have made of that?

Bonnie   Fag hanging out of mouth. She'd have said 'Elias you're a shoe-in for getting through them pearly gates'. Might drag Maggie along tomorrow. A kicking and screaming atheist, supporting her nephew.

Elias   She might catch fire.

Bonnie   Hannah said she might come.

Elias   Oh my goodness. Hope she doesn't put me off.

Bonnie   Cheering you on, I think.

They sit together in silence. There's a sense they both want to say something about **Bonnie**'s *illness.*

After a considerable amount of time, the quality of which can only be shared by mother and son, **Bonnie** *continues.*

Bonnie When my time comes. I'd like you to speak at mine.

Alina *enters in a dressing room speaking to her mother in Ukrainian.*

Alina I'm having a restful time, Mama.

Bonnie Hello Alina's mum.

Alina She says good morning.

Elias *and* **Bonnie** *leave.*

Alina *leaves.*

Scene Five: Hannah and Peter —
Easter Saturday early evening

Thunder cracks. **Hannah**, **Maggie**'s *daughter, enters. She's in a purple shell suit, tight black jeans – very much from the city.*

Hannah *ceremonially takes her shoes off and leaves them on the soil. She puts a cigarette in her mouth. Lights it.*

She moves through the kitchen, arriving at the record player.

Hannah *puts on 'Riders on the Storm' by The Doors.*

Hannah *reaches for a bottle of red wine, next to the Aga.*

Peter *enters, soaked.*

Hannah Ey, Peter! (*She goes to hug him.*)

Peter Don't come near me I'm drenched.

Hannah Oh right.

Peter moves to the Aga to start drying his clothes. **Hannah** *goes to turn off the music.*

Peter   Leave it on. One of Dad's favourites. Haven't heard it in years.

Hannah   How'd it go out there this afternoon?

Peter   We're missing a lot of ewes. Could be worse. Weird seeing them piled up like that. Full of saltwater.

Hannah   What do you need? We've got some cooking wine — oh no. You know what, I'm going to take you to the Horseshoes.

Peter   Might just stay here and attempt to get dry.

Hannah   Oh sure. Yeah yeah yeah. Mum will be back soon from her afternoon walk. You can play some Uno with Aunty Maggie.

Peter   Absolutely not.

Hannah   Pint?

They move into the Horseshoes pub, surrounded by the sounds of country pub.

Peter   If you let me drive the Tesla.

HANNAH AND PETER – IN THE PUB

They sit on the kitchen table, as if in the pub.

Peter   You realise the barman you were flirting with was Carlton?

Hannah   Oh my god, Will Carlton?

Peter   He's lost six stone and claims to be a fitness guru.

Hannah   Fuck

Peter   Truth is he had a gastric band fitted. If he has more than half a yoghurt, he shits himself.

Hannah God he must've thought I was so weird. I was talking to him like he was a stranger.

/

It's gone a bit bougie in there.

Peter It was dying on its arse. But they got a new chef in. The Americans were asking if they should come here for breakfast.

Hannah Are they a couple?

Peter No, mother and son. Well, at least I think they are.

Hannah Wow.

/

Peter They were asking how extensive the wine list is.

Hannah It's not that bougie. You never know, they might like Echo Falls.

Peter I don't think they've served rosé since the last time you cleaned them out.

Hannah Ah my god, yes. The summer of 2007.

/

Hannah Sorry I haven't. Been there. Do you know what I mean? It's just the years go by and I get distracted by what I'm achieving – no I didn't mean it like that.

Peter When Elias said you hadn't been here since pre-Covid I thought fucking hell.

Hannah I know right. I get this false sense that we've spoken. It makes me complacent about getting in touch. I was a bit nervous coming this time.

Peter Because of mum? Because it's come back.

Hannah Yeah. And that it's been so long.

Peter You are good at saying why you can't come up.

Hannah   No. Don't do that. Don't make excuses for me. You've been through it; I've not been here.

Peter   I think she's looking really. She's really on it. And I think maybe we've got more time than she's letting on and I . . .

Hannah *offers support. A long moment in silence, with only the sound of the pub. The sort of silence which can only be held by two cousins who used to be great friends.*

Hannah   One for the road?

Scene Six: Family I Easter Saturday

The whole family gather in the kitchen for the first time.

Peter *and* **Hannah** *instigate a game of wonky veg. Two teams. Two buckets on one side of the kitchen. A big pile of vegetables from the farm. It's a relay race by carrying the veg between your thighs and waddling across the kitchen and dropping the vegetables in the bucket. It's a game invented in happier times. In simpler times. The audience should feel drawn into the joy with many, many different perspectives to witness and pockets of sub-story.*

Peter   Right, it's decided before supper –

Peter and Hannah   Wonky veg game.

Peter   Hendersons vs Carters. Same rules as ever. One minute on Pingu timer.

A timer of the cartoon character Pingu is placed, alongside the veg, on the table.

Everyone *(apart from* **Peter** *and* **Hannah***) No!*

Peter and Hannah   YES.

The characters can ad lib their reactions, preparations and general thoughts about playing an old family game.

Peter *and* **Hannah** *form teams on one side of the kitchen.*

Peter   Team Carter.

Hannah   Team Henderson.

Alina   What is this game?

Maggie   Oh it's actually such a stupid game —

Peter   For Alina's benefit, Hannah please explain the rules.

Hannah   You need to collect a vegetable and run over to the bucket and drop it in the other bucket. Winner gets first dibs on seconds of pudding.

Peter   Pingu is set. Are we ready? 3-2-1 — GO

Wonky veg game happens.

We hear encouragement from both sides as well as accusations of cheating.

Peter   Right, what have you got Hendersons?

Bonnie   We've got two carrots, three potatoes and a mouldy swede.

Peter   We've got two carrots, four potatoes and a cabbage – that makes 11 points.

As the win for the Carters is celebrated, the whole family make their way to the table.

The family all take a seat at the six chairs around the table but are sat in little duets. **Alina** *is with* **Peter**, **Elias** *is with* **Hannah** *and* **Bonnie** *is with* **Maggie.**

The joy of the game descends into a concentrated exercise of painting eggs after supper.

They are all painting each other's portrait.

ALINA and PETER

Alina   Are you giving me a beard?

Peter   I am. I'm giving you a ginger bear-d.

Alina   I see. Well, I've made given you a skinhead.

ELIAS and HANNAH

Elias Do you know why we have eggs at Easter?

Hannah Er, no I don't, why?

Elias It's because Jesus, tomorrow, as it were, was inside a cave covered by a stone. And when they rolled the stone away they found that the cave was empty after he'd been crucified.

Hannah Is that the abridged version?

Elias It is.

Hannah *moves off and lays the plates on the table with chocolate cake.*

MAGGIE and BONNIE

Bonnie Oh, my word, I've made you look like mother.

Maggie Oh yes, it's the eyes!

Bonnie Why am I purple?

Maggie Why not? Purple energy today.

Bonnie My god Maggie. What on earth does that mean?

Finishing chocolate cake from the parishioners.

All quietly finishing chocolate cake. **Elias** *gives the final piece to* **Alina**.

Elias Does anyone want another slice of Dorris's cake? This is the real reason I became a priest. Easter. Cake season. The breaking of the fast.

Bonnie Mine had a dog hair in it. I'm telling you there's half a Labrador in there, I reckon.

Alina I propose a toast. To Dorris? (*Cheers in Ukrainian*)

Bonnie *goes and gets the annual general meeting paperwork in a folder. She has the minutes from last year, the agenda, the end of year accounts and so on.*

Act One: EASTER 2025, Scene Six

Bonnie Right, sorry this is the boring bit of the evening now. Year-end draft, now you should've had this by email. But here you go. You give some of them out Pete. We can jump to item three. The figures. Pete, you could talk us through this.

Peter So if you turn to page 11, I think, yes you can all see the bottom line for the year is red, with those brackets around the number. Now that's obviously not great news in terms of this year and next. And, with the cashflow updates I've been giving you, we're still unfortunately, deep-ish into the overdraft — but find me a farmer who's not in their overdraft. One of the standouts is the brewery which is doing well. Thanks to Elias. Doug's IPA is flying off the shelf. Airbnb's busy enough. Couldn't believe how booked we were in the winter, considering how wet it's been.

The new lambing shed is proving invaluable . . . thanks to the loan from Aunty Maggie – no repayments possible yet – but once we start getting the money in for the lamb in Q2 of next year, things are looking better. We're exploring other ways to maximise profits from the sheep. So milk, cheese, soap and . . . sorry that's a bit all over the place in terms of order of things, is that ok?

Elias Well done Peter.

Bonnie What you haven't got here of course is the cost from this week's storm damage – loss of livestock. And the wheat and barley yields are down, that's because it was so wet last spring, wasn't it? And there's something else you need think about going forward. If you turn back to page six, Alina – can you explain what you've been working on.

Alina Yes, so if you turn to page 6 you can see the report on the soil samples I've taken over the year.

As you can see, the quality is depreciating. Look, like dust to touch in some fields. And this, this is what it should be like. Like Dorris's cake, only more worms. We cannot keep growing crops here — only plants that feed the soil.

Bonnie And this from 72 Acres?

Alina Yes, the ones with no hedges suffer more. I'm sorry it is not better news.

Bonnie Well, I think we all agree, we're going to have to talk to Ron about this. So, item three. Proposed budget for this year. The RPA money is being phased out by April '27. And despite the end of the tenancy in sight, the landlord is hiking rent up in line with inflation. We saw that coming. But don't forget with Labour wading in with their new policies, who knows where they'll be putting the goalposts. So, the budget for this year coming, is going to be a struggle to break even again. Plus, I'm sorry someone's got to say this. You're not going to have me. You're going to have a 50 per cent reduction in workforce next year.

Peter *leaves. It's too much for him to contemplate this.*

Bonnie We don't have the reserves Pete to keep —

Alina *follows. Followed by* **Hannah**. *Followed by* **Elias**. *The younger generation have all gone, leaving the two sisters.*

Bonnie I need everyone here so we can talk about this really.

Maggie, when I die, that's it, that tenancy is up. And that could be by Christmas. Pete can't deal with this on his own. He's already flat out as is. He's thirty-seven and he already looks like Doug, don't he? And if Pete is serious about trying to buy this place, he's got to be realistic. Yes, he knows how to fix a rotavator, but he also needs to understand the figures. You see these days Maggie – it's not enough to just be a farmer.

Bonnie *is very upset. She slams down the accounts on the table.*

Maggie *stands and goes to her.* **Maggie** *sits by her sister, soothing her.*

Bonnie *places a toy tractor in front of her, and* **Maggie** *rests her head on the table.* **Bonnie** *rests her head on the table. They stare at each other. Eventually a smile comes out.*

These two sisters are back at the farmhouse table as children, a simpler time.

Scene Seven: Danny and Darren – Easter Saturday morning

*The relative calm and quiet is disrupted, rapidly, by the sound of **Danny** and **Darren**'s drum and bass in their Transit van. The sound roars and then cuts into:*

RIDING OUT

Danny *and* **Darren** *are in the front of the Transit van, preparing for their day of collecting fallen livestock.*

Darren   Where to first then my little taxi driver?

Danny   We got seventy chicken carcasses savaged by foxes in Loddon, two lame llamas at Banham Zoo, ten piglets at Castle Acre —

Darren   — What happened at Banham Zoo?

Danny   Two llamas had a fight.

Darren   Oh right.

Danny   Then two heifers in Docking and then we're back next door.

Darren   Next door?

Danny   Ewes on the salt marsh.

Darren   Peter Carter's grazing sheep on the salt marsh? Fucking hell. How long's he been doing that?

Danny   Thought you knew. Been doing it since you were inside.

Darren   He didn't have a flock when he put me away.

/

They can't leave us alone, can they? Stealing our land, our ideas.

Danny Dad does cattle Darren.

Darren Yeah, we do cattle Danny, we been doing it for years. We've been on the marsh for years. National Trust *trust* us, don't they. And then that Peter getting in there with his desperate —

Danny — He's just doing black Horns.

Darren — Heritage n' all. Fucking hell.

/

Danny You jealous then.

Darren Nah. He's failing, isn't he? Anyway. Sheep? In Norfolk. Like lambs to the slaughter.

They drive for some time.

Danny Is that a tattoo of a cross?

Darren Crucifix, little boi. Found Jesus now. Ben Gilly. My cell mate. In prison – helped me see the light. Showed me the way. Gave me this a few months ago.

/

Danny Right.

/

Darren I'm changed now little brother. I have

Danny Ok, well if you're changed can you give Stacey a call. She's being a pain in moi arse.

Darren Can't go near her now. She's a sinner.

Danny What?

/

Darren Stop off at the Gulf garage. I want a Snickers, then I wanna look out at the sea. Then I wanna watch the Oystercatchers floating on the thermals.

Danny Right. Then we gotta do some work.

PETROL FILLING STATION

Darren Long old day my little brother. Big old Norfolk loop. Stinks in the back.

Danny Right, I'll drop you at mum's. I'll do the ewes on Peter's marsh.

Darren No, I'll come. It'll be alright. I'll help.

Danny You can't go near can ya?

Darren Fuck the restraining order. Fuck Graham in Norwich. Fuck parole officers with the Hugo Boss stink. Parasites. No one is the fucking boss of me.

Danny Right. Well, I'm dropping you at mum's. She's made your tea. I've got the winch. I'll be fine.

RIDING OUT II

Darren Happy Easter, my little brother.

Danny *hands* **Darren** *an Easter egg.*

Darren No thanks.

Danny You alright?

Darren Yep. Where'd you go then last night?

Danny The Bluebell. Bangin' time.

Darren That's a long way to go for a pint.

Danny Jimmy's lost his licence, not going to get the Coasthopper, is he?

Darren Who else was there?

Danny Kelcey and Steve for a bit.

Darren Why did you leave?

Danny Pub closed.

Darren Fair.

Danny And I was tired. Hauled the dead ewes in the back on my own, didn't I? Wanted to go home. What about you? You watch tele with mum?

Darren Nope. Got on my knees. Said my prayers and then went to bed, didn't I? 'For God so loved the world that gave his only son. For whosoever believeth in him shall not perish but have everlasting life'. John 3.16. That's my bangin' time now.

Danny Right.

Scene Eight: Rachel and Bartlett in the windmill

Bartlett *and* **Rachel** *are on a balcony at the top of the windmill. They are relaxing with a bottle of red wine, overlooking the farm.*

Bartlett Mom. What's the farmer called?

Rachel Peter.

Bartlett Peter's screaming at the moon.

Rachel I heard him this afternoon. Poor lamb. God that shower is so, so bad.

/

Rachel Hey, would you look at that, I can see the Big Dipper!

Bartlett Here they called it the Plough.

Rachel Oh cute. No, I can see what they say about the big Norfolk skies. You don't get that in Norwich, Vermont.

Act One: EASTER 2025, Scene Eight

Bartlett And tomorrow you've got the lambing experience. And you're actually gonna, you know stick your hand up a sheep's —

Rachel Vagina?

Bartlett Gross.

/

Bartlett Well. my morning's decided. The Deus II metal detector is fully charged and ready to find some Roman coins.

Rachel In this mud?

Bartlett Maybe I'll find my gold.

Rachel I just wanna see some new life. Life, Bart. The potential here is incredible, don't you think?

Bartlett They're missing a trick. Jurassic Coast: East. You know in Happisburgh they found the oldest footprints in Europe? What people want is the fun. They just don't know what is under our feet. You could have a Dinoland theme park with eco lodges. You could have coaches of tourists streaming in. All these fields with sugar beet. Such a waste of land. You could turn it into a Bronze Age world with the mud huts and you pay regional actors to play the people.

Rachel Actors? What are you talking about? They've already got a brewery here. That is, of course, until Adnams takes over! Or what about a writer's retreat?

Bartlett That's nice — so you have a retreat that's like ten people on it and they're paying $2,000 a time.

Rachel Don't you just love prospecting? How many acres is it? What, 500?

Bartlett Maybe more.

Rachel You know you could strip it bare and start again. Start with an art gallery. Obviously. We could import the pots from Kyoto. And a vineyard over there. Grow a lovely Pinot. There's a lot of money up here and I think they could raise the money, but I don't think they have the vision.

Bartlett Oh, I see your game. This is what the divorce settlement is for?!

Rachel It's your heritage sweety. Your grandfather would've looked down from the sky on those same salt marshes not knowing if it was his last day on earth –

Bartlett -I know, mom. Lancaster bombers, RAF Bacton. The War.

Rachel I'm proud of him, Bart. You should be too.

/

Bartlett You know there's a 'For Sale' sign up by the other entrance?

Rachel What? Are they selling? How much?

Scene Nine: Elias, Alina, Bonnie (and Peter) — Easter Sunday morning 8am

Easter Sunday. The farm kitchen. Radio 4 news plays in the background. Reports of further rains and flooding nationwide.

Elias *and* **Alina** *are having breakfast.*

Alina *is sat with her microscope. In the video design, we can see a close-up of what is under the microscope.*

Elias *is sat working on his sermon. Periodically he stands up and goes to the microphone.*

Alina *speaks to her mum in Ukrainian – chatting about her grandmother.*

Elias *says in Happy Easter in Ukrainian.*

Elias *continues his personal preparation.*

Elias On this Easter morning I'd like us to all think about . . . Easter as a symbol of new life. It is fragile, and yet strong. It is a place where human life begins.

Sits again muttering to himself.

Bonnie *walking in on the phone to* **Ron**, *the agronomist.*

Bonnie Yes. Yes they did say that. Very high, I think. Oh, alright Ron, that's good to know. No problem. Tuesday is fine. Ok. Ok Ron, love to Martha. Ok.

Sits down at the kitchen table.

Bonnie Right, you two. I was going to wait for Peter but he's still out there, knee-deep.

Bonnie *takes two little Easter eggs out of her pocket. One each for* **Elias** *and* **Alina**.

Elias Happy Easter.

Alina My favourite. Creme Egg.

Bonnie What are you up to there? Oh, is that the soil in Three Trees field?

Alina No this is a sample from the soil nursery at the science research park. This is Three Trees.

They look together.

Bonnie It's brilliant this gizmo. You are so clever. I have no idea what that is, things wiggling about. Is that bacteria in the soil?

Alina Yes, these are actinomycetes. They help decompose the organic matter in the soil. It's what helps give the soil that lovely earthy smell. It's my favourite bacteria. This is the sample of 72 Acres, in front of the house.

Bonnie Oh dear. Nothing wiggling around in that. So, I'm guessing 72 Acres has seen better days?

Elias So, the saltwater has taken a lot of the life?

Aline Yes. These bacteria are very sensitive to waterlogged conditions. So, the sea water ingress will be killing the soil. It's becoming more of a problem now the floods are more frequent – and the old ditches are not up to the job.

They look.

Alina What was the soil like after the flood in 1983?

Bonnie Oh. I mean Ron, actually it was your dad, Elias. Well let's be honest, we all just merrily bunged a load of fertiliser on there and it was back. The crops came back. The fields were very resilient then.

Alina And the water level this time is higher or lower?

Bonnie It's a bit higher this time, I think. You can see where it got to in this photo.

(*To Elias.*)

This is 1983. Your dad built a little flint wall to show where the water got to. Even though it was in the middle of the field. That's the watermark.

Elias Is *that* what that is?? I genuinely didn't know that.

Bonnie Oh yes, he insisted that if we put a little wall up, it'd turn away the tide. Like a Norfolk King Canute, Doug was. Whereas Ron's just told us to bung a load of fertiliser on it —

Alina - Is Ron saying the same now?

Bonnie Yeah. He's been saying the same for the last thirty-five years.

Alina It looks like there used to be some hedges.

Bonnie Yeah, we took those out in the mid-eighties. That's what everyone was doing, see. Bigger fields. Bigger machines. Bigger yields. That's why it's now called 72 Acres. It used to be four smaller fields.

Elias *is up in his sermon position on a microphone.*

Elias And the way to life stands open. In our saviour Jesus Christ, Amen.

Peter *enters the kitchen.*

Peter Morning, morning, morning. Christ is risen!

All Morning Peter/Pete.

Peter You know that scatty ewe in bay four?

Bonnie Yeah.

Peter She's only gone and had triplets.

Bonnie No!

Peter Taken to them really well.

Bonnie Didn't think she had it in her.

Peter That's gotta be worth a cream egg?

Bonnie *hands* **Peter** *an Easter egg.*

Bonnie She did all the work.

Peter Well, I'll make sure I'll share it with her. Tradition states, we're not to eat our eggs until after Easter lunch has been overcooked.

Peter *turns to* **Elias.**

I'll come along later.

Elias Yeah?

Peter Yeah. I fancy saying a prayer. Managed to find cover. Forty-five minutes, is it? The Hendersons up?

Bonnie No, no. They're on London hours.

Scene Nine, Part II

During which the Easter Sunday lunch is being cleared away.

34 Black Sheep

Hannah *is frantically trying to get ready to join the rest of the Carters at church.* **Maggie** *is making coffee by the Aga.*

Hannah   Why didn't you wake me?

Maggie   Coffee?

Hannah   I'll drive.

Maggie   Well, I'm not going.

Hannah   What? You are going. We have to go, mum.

Maggie   I'm cooking lunch, you go.

Hannah   You're not going to go support? That's a bold move.

Scene Ten: Family II

The family are all around the table. They are nattering over each other, each with a little line/thought about the service **Elias** *has just led.*

Bonnie   I loved that bit where you talked / about new life

Peter   I wouldn't / put money on the plate by I only had / 10p in my pocket!

Alina   Good singing / at the end there Bonnie.

Hannah *arrives in the scene.*

Hannah   Guys, guys, pre-lunch Pictionary?

Hannah *leads on Pictionary playing.*

Hannah   I've got the paper. Youngsters vs Oldies, and Elias.

Peter   Ok timer at the ready. Go.

Hannah *start to draw, then* **Peter**.

Peter   Hills. Tour de France.

Alina   King?

Peter Sun?

Alina Kong.

/

Peter *Lion King*!

Hannah Yes!

Peter Ok I'll go.

Hannah Well, that's not really the rules, but sure.

Peter Ok Ok. (**Peter** *starts to draw.*)

Time slows.

Bonnie *steps away from the scene. Watches in, moving around the kitchen. The game has triggered her to think about* **Doug**, *her husband, and the dad of* **Peter** *and* **Elias**.

Bonnie Hello Doug. Can't believe it's been ten years without you, my love. I wish you could've been there today. Elias was wondering. Pete was there too — he's really turned out to be a right chip off the old block. It's been just lovely having them all around me this Easter. Watching them all joking and arguing and going to the pub. Just normal stuff. Yeah. Normal life. I am a bit scared Doug.

Elias *senses his mum is leaving them. He gets up from his seat and supports her, brings her back into the kitchen.*

But I can't put that on the boys. So here I am talking to you.

Elias *leads her back to her seat.*

Hannah Jungle Book?!

The timer goes off. **Peter** *is furious.*

Peter NO. It's Alanis Morissette! That's a guitar.

Alina I thought that was an orangutan.

Peter Fine.

Hannah Shall we play another game.

I was, I was thinking about last night and maybe we could go again with that discussion. We've got this game we play at work. It's fun. It's called 'Agree/Disagree', do you wanna play?

Bonnie Go on then, a game from work.

Hannah So, if you stand here right, you 'Strongly Agree' with the statement and this end is 'Strongly Disagree' with the statement. Got it?

And then you can stand in between.

For example, if I was to say to you. 'The lamb was perfectly cooked'. Where would you stand?

The family all move to 'Strongly Agree', apart from **Peter** *who stands at the 'Strongly Disagree'.*

Bonnie You ate it!

Peter Course I ate it. It's my lamb!

Hannah *offers another statement. She's really commanding the game now, perhaps in a way she hasn't done before with the family. She checks her notes, in her notebook.*

Hannah 'I love being in the house with everyone'.

They all move to 'Strongly Agree'.

Bonnie I should hope so.

Hannah 'This land makes my heart sing'.

They move to a real mixture of positions. **Bonnie** *and* **Maggie** *in sync.*

Hannah 'I want to try to buy the farm from Mr Young'.

Maggie, **Bonnie** *move to 'Strongly Disagree', the younger generation stay with 'Strongly Disagree'.*

Hannha 'I have a solution for how to do that'.

Act One: EASTER 2025, Scene Ten   37

They all move to 'Strongly Disagree', apart from **Hannah** *who moves to 'Strongly Agree'.*

Peter Go on then.

Hannah *prepares herself.*

Hannah I think it's entirely possible. Right?

But I think we need to make a proposal. I think what this farm needs. I think if we stepped away . . . If we focused on . . . oh god, ok. What if we turned this place into a teaching farm?

Right? Tried to buy 100 acres of it. Built a place where kids from the city could come and learn about the land. Four-day residencies. Big bookings. Alina could work with them. Outdoor learning. Aunty B. Aunty B — I know this is not your world. But it's my world. I could really, really help with the partnerships. I think we could make this place part of the community again, and not an island of . . . pain.

Peter It's not farming though. Is it?

Alina It would help regenerate the soil, Peter.

Hannah It is farming.

Peter Is it?

Hannah It is.

Peter *leaves again.* **Alina** *follows.*

Hannah Mum?

Maggie Hannah. I hear, I love everything you've said. I'm so sorry we haven't discussed this before. I just want to say that I will do anything I can to help, but I do want to be guided by what Bonnie wants.

Elias Bonnie is here. So, what does Bonnie want? What do you want mum?

Bonnie I want to go for a walk.

Bonnie *exits.*

Peter *re-enters in a rush.*

Peter Sorry I keep fucking off. And Alina said . . . I just keep feeling like I'm being threatened, when everyone is being really kind . . . is Elias with mum?

Hannah Yeah —

Peter Why don't we just sit down and look at it again tomorrow.

Hannah, **Peter** *and* **Maggie** *are left in the kitchen.*

Scene Eleven: Danny and Elias – Easter Sunday evening

The church.

Elias *is sat in the pew on his own.*

Danny *enters, watching* **Elias** *fondly.*

Elias *doesn't see him. Then after some time.*

Danny How was it?

Elias It went really well. Really well. Fifty five turned up. Big date in the diary. The weeks of preparation. Sleepless nights. And then whoosh, hallelujah, He's risen. On to Christmas.

They hug.

Danny Do you not get stage fright? I'd be terrified standing up in front of all those people.

Elias No. No, I love it.

Danny Oh, wait, close your eyes. Sit down. Hands out. (*He puts an Easter egg in his hands.* **Elias** *opens his eyes.*) Darren didn't want it.

Elias Charming! Thanks! So. How is he?

Danny Was Darren here today?

Elias In church?

Danny He's found god now. When he was inside. Got this huge tattoo of a crucifix on his arm. He says Easter is nothing but eating chocolate eggs these days.

Elias Oh yeah? (**Elias** *offers Danny an egg.*)

Danny Thanks. (**Danny** *eats the egg.*)

I can't wait for the summer. My dad's got a little dinghy at Moreston. We could take it out. See the seals?

Elias I'll have to check my diary. Yep, I'm free.

Danny Am I allowed to kiss you in church?

Elias It's practically forbidden not to.

They do.

Scene Twelve: Bonnie, Peter and Elias

The farm kitchen. Easter Monday.

Peter *enters listening to Radio 4. He's looking at a baby monitor keeping an eye on the labs.*

Bonnie *enters.* **Maggie** *and* **Hannah** *have left.*

Bonnie I love my sister — but they are exhaustin'. Took them an hour to leave.

Peter Hannah's fun. We can chuck out that oat milk now though.

/

I saw the Americans running together down Chalkpit Lane.

Bonnie Yeah, I saw 'em in their matching outfits.

/

Peter Am I doing that thing with the mother?

Bonnie Rachel. Yeah. She does know what it entails?

/

Peter Can you ever see us doing that?

Bonnie Running?

Peter A family holiday . . . together. Matching outfits.

Elias *enters.*

Bonnie Last holiday I had was 1997. Long weekend in Southwold — never again.

/

Where does Hannah get these ideas from?

Why does she think that's what I wanna hear?

Peter As if Mr Young would split up the farm. What are you supposed to do with 100 acres. It's all thought-showers, mind-maps and spider diagrams.

Bonnie It's nonsense. She comes up here, what, six days a year. The idea of Maggie being out of London.

Peter Do you think she was annoyed about the loan? She had seen the figures.

Bonnie No. She's not tight, Maggie. I know she's only trying to help. She's thinking it's what Doug would want. But I don't know. I've been turning it all over this weekend. And. Me and your dad we both worked ourselves into early graves. I don't want that for you. We took this farm on because that's what you did. It's what our parents expected. But you've got choices, boys. But I'm not going to do that to you. I'm not going to do what grandpops did to me.

The tenancy is coming to an end Pete. That's a chance to get out.

Peter This is our farm mum.

Bonnie Peter, look at the bank balance. Look at the state of the soil. Look at the state of everyone farming around here. BPS's gone money. Instead, these endless bloody environmental grants that even if you get them pay you peanuts. And that subsidy is pushing us further and further and further way from this (*she picks up some soil*). And this. (*She picks up a toy tractor*). And this. (*she picks up a carrot*) to what?

Oh, that's right. Lovely wildflowers and nothing to eat.

You're a young man Pete. Let someone else worry about it.

God knows, we've done our time.

Elias Three generations of Carters.

Bonnie Eighty bloody years.

/

Peter So, you won't be lambing with Rachel then?

Bonnie No, I'm going to get a pint of normal milk.

Bonnie *leaves.* **Elias** *tries to continue the conversation with* **Peter.**

Elias *takes a handful of soil.*

Elias You know, I've been thinking Peter —

Peter — Put that soil back.

/

Elias You don't need to do on your own.

Peter I don't need a sermon, Elias.

Elias We could do this togeth —

Peter *explodes.*

Peter PUT IT BACK!!

Peter *has lost his cool.* **Elias** *runs away, shocked.*

Peter *gathers all the soil into a neat pile on the table. As per the very opening of the story.*

Scene Thirteen: A lamb is born

Radio music plays in the lambing shed.

Rachel   Peter! Peter

Peter   Ah you must be Rachel. I'll turn that radio down. Your son joining us?

Rachel   He's busy right now. Detecting.

Peter   Ok, so this is the mum.

Peter *takes hold of one of the straw bales, which is generally used as the sheep or any livestock in the story.*

You just missed her having her first.

Rachel   Oh no, that's too bad, I'm so sorry.

Peter   That's fine she's got another one in there. You see the lamb shaking its head, which is a good sign, getting all that gunk out and the yellow staining on the lamb's fleece is from the lamb pooping in the amniotic fluid before birth.

Rachel   Oh Christ.

Elias *enters and begins his Eulogy for* **Bonnie.**

Scene Fourteen: Bonnie's Eulogy

The church, six months on.

Elias   A warm welcome to you all this afternoon. I'd like to say a huge thank you to you all outside, surrounding St Thomas's. I'm sorry we couldn't fit you all in. But thank you to Danny Dixon for linking up a last-minute speaker outside. So, you should be able to hear us. In fact, if you can hear us can you give us a cheer, on the count of three. One, two, three

There's a huge cheer and whoops from outside. The entire farming community has turned up for **Bonnie**'*s funeral.*

Act One: EASTER 2025, Scene Fourteen 43

Great. So, to many of you, she was Bonnie. Or Mrs Carter. To some of you she might have been that kind face at the fish and chip shop. To others, a warm presence, radiating from Oyster Catcher Farm. To me and Peter of course, she was mum. And I'm so pleased that the sun is shining today. Mum was hoping that today would be a celebration – a party. And insisted that anyone that came along, had a chance to hear about her wild days. Her love of the film *The Matrix* and Keanu Reeves. And she wanted me to share her the love of cricket. And in particular, the West Indian fast bowler. In fact, there's a long list of very mum like requests in the vestry, if you'd like to take a look.

Mum spent most of her childhood here. And I remember our Granny, Granny P telling us that mum was in the tractor, solo, from the age of seven. To Granny's horror, early one spring morning, she looked out the window and saw that Mum was ploughing a ginormous 'X' in the field. And when Granny P ran out and confronted her. Picture the scene. Mum simply mumbled under her breath 'I wanted to put a kiss on the land. To wish it luck for the growing season. And to show the aliens where they can land if they want to'. An imagination reaching across galaxies. Even at a young age.

And in her teenage years, mum along with her sister Maggie, would regularly be seen being chucked out of the Plough pub at closing time. After a long summer's evening of drinking together, sharing pints. No doubt on their way to a famous Norfolk rave. And never one to waste a pint. Mum would drive them back to our farm. And mum would be holding a pint out of the window, trying not to spill a drop. She told me that she'd never laughed so hard – and that she had sore ribs for three weeks.

Those pint glasses are still on our windowsill. Trophies of summers gone by. Fast forward into her late twenties when me and Peter came along. Mum started this new tradition at harvest time. She insisted on having a photo with us in the tractor in the field, from the exact same angle. Capturing us from being tiny babies, to toddlers, teenagers, young men and onwards. All the way to the harvest on our farm this year. It's a timelapse. Of how we changed but also how she changed. And the image of Peter sat on mum's lap, aged thirty-eight, and the laughter on their faces, is a moment that I think, I think she'll be taking with her into everlasting rest.

Now mum said that she didn't mind either way, if her illness was mentioned. And part of me thought it'd be best to just etch that from her story. But actually, you know, both times when she was ill. I learnt, we learnt so much from her. And I wouldn't describe her response as strength. More of a staring competition with her mortality. And as she said to us both, just before she passed. 'You've got to stare at life's problem's, boys. Soften your eyes. Open your heart. And remember, remember to always listen to nature. Because it will tell you everything you need to know'.

Amen.

Interval.

Act Two: EASTER 2026

Scene Fifteen: A village hall, close to the farm

The auditorium, usually as the village hall, is fully lit. There is some background music playing.

Tea, biscuits have been handed out. A chatty, bright atmosphere.

Heather, *a farming succession facilitator from Yorkshire, is making her way through the audience, making small talk.* **Heather** *should always be played by the same actor who played* **Bonnie**.

There's a microphone, maybe a flipchart.

As she's walking through the auditorium, you begin to hear her talking.

Heather   I think we're close to getting started, aren't we? Have we all had a cup of tea and a bun? And had a wee. Right. It's nice to see some familiar faces. Don't worry I'm not going to do any karaoke.

Hannah, **Peter**, **Alina** *and* **Elias** *all make their way into the auditorium and take a seat.*

Right, we better get cracking, otherwise we're going to be here all day.

Oh, hang on they've asked me to use one of these.

Heather *starts using the microphone.*

How's that? Oh, it's like *Stars in Their Eyes*, isn't it? Thanks so much everyone for giving up your Good Friday to be here. For those of you that don't know me, my name is Heather Bagnall. And my official title is Succession Facilitator, which you might have googled. But I like to think of myself as a farming business counsellor.

Tonight, as we unpick our problems as farmers, we'll probably talk about succession, finances, legal problems, tax, tenancy – but my focus is always on people. On you.

Little bit of background about me, so you know I'm not just a random person who's come in to keep warm. I grew up on my family's farm in the North West. My dad's retired now and my brother's running the farm. And you know when I was young, I left to go travelling, did a bit of contract farming abroad, and when I came home, I noticed how bloody miserable people in my community were. How terrible farmers are at talking to each other. Especially about their problems, or, god forbid, about the future. So, I did a Nuffield scholarship on succession and change in agriculture, and twenty years later, basically here I am. So, I'll give you a fact to start with. Did you know, one in four farming families aren't speaking to each other? If you've experienced that, I know I have, you're not on your own.

It's difficult, when your business partners are also your loved ones.

How many CEOs have to deal with that? Well, Trump, I suppose. But let's not waste our breath on him.

Farming is a unique business isn't it, because it's also your history, your identity, your family, your purpose, your home as well as your livelihood. It's hard. But famers are used to doing difficult things, right?

So, I'm just here to help start some conversations. I'm going to start by – it's called taking the temperature of the room – which sounds medical – but I've just got a few questions for everyone. It's come up from the issues I've been hearing around the country.

So, if you could help by a show of hands, that'd be great.

So, if I start by asking. How many people would prefer to buy their food from British producers?

How many would that be?

Heather *reacts.*

What if I asked, how many people think they are dealing with the sharp end of climate change? **Heather** *reacts.*

How many people feel that the unpredictability of farming is really stressful?

Heather *reacts.*

Something that's specific to where we are now. How many people are coming to the end of their tenancy, and don't know if they want to carry on farming?

There's a couple. Yeah. And I was having some chat before we came in, over a hot crossed bun. Can I put you on the spot, if you don't mind?

Yeah? Oh, the exciting thing is I've got a microphone for you as well, love. We could do a duet if you want.

Peter No thanks!

Heather Does it work?

Peter Yes. I don't think I've performed in this village hall for thirty years. *Jack and the Beanstalk.* Bailiff One.

Heather I can see there's a few people who remember that. Was he any good?

Peter I think I was the tallest in the year. I think that's why I got the role. Anyway. We were talking a little outside, yes and we've been through it. We lost our mum tail end of last year and, well, we've just lost our farm.

Heather You've lost your farm.

Peter Yes. Third-generation leasehold. Let down by my aunty. She has the opportunity to buy it from the owner. But she wanted to stay in her townhouse in North London.

Hannah *speaks up from the back.*

Hannah Well, that's not totally fai —

Peter Well, you can speak in a minute Hannah. We've done our last harvest; we're wrapping things up . . .

Heather What's your name darling?

Peter Peter Carter.

Heather *Have you got other family members here?*

Peter We're a sort of conga line going back through the hall. We've got my brother Elias here. He's an excellent part-time farmer. Alina's been fantastic, we've had a lot of soil issues. Anyway, probably time for me to move on.

Heather Just before you do Peter, can I ask, have you accepted that your farm is finished?

Peter Our hopes for the farm died with mum. Everywhere you go it reminds us of her. Maybe it's easier to just have a fresh start.

Heather Can you see yourself as a farmer at in the future, Peter?

Peter Maybe, working for a big estate where there's structure, support, holiday. Where it doesn't always feel like it's you by yourself.

Heather That's such a big point you've raised there. That feeling of being alone when you're working really long hours. You're under so much pressure. All that anxiety. It's going to take a big toll on your mental health. It's great you've recognised that. I'm seeing some nods of people who've been through something similar.

Peter You're nodding away Elias, do you want to say something?

Heather It's alright no-one has to speak, if they don't want to.

Elias *leaves.* **Alina** *follows.* **Peter** *leaves too.*

Hannah *takes hold of the microphone.*

Hannah Elias has just taken a bit of a battering there, maybe they'll come back.

Heather Well, it's emotional isn't it – talking about it – issues of succession often arise when you're also dealing with the loss of a family member. When you're grieving. How are you feeling about it Hannah?

Hannah Well, I did make a proposal to buy some of the land. To try to do a teaching farm. To try to keep the family on the farm.

And it didn't work. We needed the funds quickly for that to go through and we couldn't do it. Some of the family want to stay, others don't. It's been sold to some real outsiders —

Heather — Outsiders?

Hannah Yes, some Americans. Um, developers, I think.

Heather I see.

Hannah The rest of the family all want out. I'm trying to work out how and if I can stay in some capacity.

/

Heather So, you have the support of the rest of the family, if you want to stay?

Hannah I don't know. And also, with all the grief lying around. I don't know if I have to have their support.

*We see **Elias** and **Alina** enter the farm kitchen, behind where **Heather** is stood. **Elias** and **Alina** are arguing, de-voiced so we don't hear what they are saying, but it's a passionate discussion.*

I was wondering if you've ever come across this, in your work?

Heather Absolutely, Hannah. It's so common. Especially when you've got a third-generation tenancy coming to an end. Often the younger generation are very divided about what they want to do. Some family members just want to sell the assets, cash up and get out. Others want to keep the family history. This is the emotional nightmare of tenancy farming.

So, what I'm going to say to you is that I'm afraid you've just got to be really business like about it. Yeah? I assume the Americans have bought some of the assets; machinery and what have you. Go home. Tot up what's left, work out what it's worth, sell it, give everybody their portion they're entitled to. And that's it. You have no more ties.

Then you do what you want to do.

Rachel *walks into the kitchen behind* **Heather**.

So, I think you take your ideas to the Americans. Fulfil your vision Hannah – all you can do is ask. Come on, give me that (**Heather** *takes the microphone from* **Hannah**)

There you go. Step back into that farm kitchen.

Hannah *stands on the edge of the farm kitchen.*

Scene Sixteen: Rachel and Bartlett with Hannah

Hannah *takes a deep breath and steps into the farm kitchen. It's full of packing boxes. Much of the life, the character of the farm kitchen has been dismantled, taken away.*

Rachel *and* **Bartlett** *are prowling around the kitchen.*

Rachel There you are. So good of you to come say hello. You remember Bart, don't you?

Hannah I do. Good to see you again. Sorry about the mess and the cross over. God this house. I used to chew the ends of this table. Anyway, don't mind me I'm just making a cuppa.

Elias *walks through with boxes.*

Rachel Please. Go right ahead. Oh my goodness you're all so busy and we're right in the way.

Act Two: EASTER 2026, Scene Sixteen

Hannah   It's an exciting time for you guys.

Rachel   Oh, I must admit, I'm exhausted. I need a holiday.

Hannah   So, it looks like you have some plans there. You mind, if I ask?

Rachel   Oh, no, not at all. We've had lots of discussions.

Bartlett   I took a little convincing.

Rachel   I mean the thing is — this farming thing has been done. And now. It's time for something new.

Hannah   Right.

Bartlett   Tell her mom.

Bartlett *spreads out the title deed across the kitchen table, followed by a large piece of tracing paper which outlines significant new plans for the land.*

Rachel   Well. I love a Pinot. So, we're going to grow some lovely grapes and we're going to make a wine!

Bartlett   Wine is perfect for this quality of soil. But we can't do this on our own.

Rachel   That's right. We need someone who's familiar.

Bartlett   Someone we trust.

Rachel   We really like you, Hannah. We think you're great. Would you come and work with us?

/

Bartlett   Mom has a lot of commitments back home. And I need someone to work alongside me in tandem. And we want that to be a local and who better – than a Carter.

Rachel   Estate manager.

Hannah   Wow. Yes. I mean. Do you have any other plans?

Bartlett We'll start with a Pinot and then after that. Much more.

Bartlett We'll also be looking at the pottery, smokehouse and the gallery. And there might be an opportunity for a writer's retreat, yoga studio.

/

Hannah Have you thought about retaining some land for . . . for a teaching farm?

Bartlett I'm sorry can you – a teaching farm? That sounds like . . .

Rachel/Bartlett Farming!

Hannah Yes, it does, doesn't it? In terms of your role in the community. You could have residencies. Kids from all over the country could come and learn from the land.

Rachel That's so cute. Especially coming from, you're Bonnie's daughter, right?

Hannah Niece.

Bartlett So, we have a Carter on board?

Hannha Henderson, but can I take this away to have a look?

Barlett Sure. This is a draft contract. It gives you an indication of starting salary. Health insurance. You'd live on site, if you choose. The windmill would be at your disposal. You know, perks.

Hannah To be continued.

Hannah *leaves into the farmyard.*

Bartlett That went well. Although she's British so maybe we should add dental.

Elias *enters with a moving box in his arms.*

Act Two: EASTER 2026, Scene Seventeen   53

Elias Out with the old. Sorry I don't think I introduced myself. I'm Elias.

Bartlett Henderson.

Elias Cart/er

Bartlett Carter. Sure. This is my mother, Rachel.

Rachel So nice to meet you.

Elias See this table. Those notches here. That was my height when I could first stand up by myself.

Bartlett Well, it will make a fine addition to your new kitchen.

They all stand in silence.

Elias Oh. I think I'd like it to stay here, actually.

Rachel So kind.

Bartlett What a lovely gesture.

Bartlett *and* **Rachel** *begin to exit, leaving* **Elias** *alone in the kitchen.*

Bartlett I was speaking to the district council, and I can't get through to the person I need to speak to.

Scene Seventeen: Darren and Elias in church

Elias *sits on the church pew.*

Darren *enters to begin his C of E learning session with* **Elias.**

Darren *is holding a copy of the King James Bible.*

Elias It's the big stories you have to be able to recite first.

Darren Like?

Elias Well, from the beginning.

Darren Yeah Genesis to the Proverbs. I've got my favourite passages, haven't I?

Elias I know you do! You recite them to me whenever you can.

Darren Yep.

Elias But knowing where the Old Testament fits in the context with other faiths. So, Cain and Abel.

Darren — A farmer and a shepherd —

Elias — For example, in Islam it's broadly the same story. So, there's some common ground there, which is wonderful.

Darren *has moved up to the microphone.*

Darren How long does it take then? Before you cun be one, a vicar I mean. You were at uni last I heard?

Elias Yes. I studied something else.

Darren Oh yeah. What was that?

Elias Philosophy.

Darren At a posh uni was it? Like that school you went to.

Elias Quite posh yeah. But you know that I'm not posh.

Darren You sound posh? Everyone from that school was posh.

Elias Were they?

Darren Yep.

Elias But Darren your family has more money than ours.

Darren Do we?

Elias Well, your family owns all your farm, don't you?

Darren We do.

Elias Well, we're tenants Darren, in our overdraft for six years straight.

Darren Yeah, I know Elias. I know. Still got a Tesla in the yard, though, haven't you?

Act Two: EASTER 2026, Scene Seventeen

Elias My aunty is a lawyer.

Darren Now, that's a true sinner.

/

Elias Darren.

Darren What?

Elias You need to try to keep god's word . . .

Darren God's word what?

Elias It's ok.

Darren No go on . . .

Elias God's word. God's word as just a guide.

Darren What so you, you don't believe what's written down there.

Elias No, I do. But there has to be some flexibility.

Darren They teach you that on your philosophy course, did they?

Danny *enters*.

Danny Hello. You almost don —

Darren — oh hello Danny. Didn't expect to see you here.

Danny Came to pick you up.

Darren How'd you know I was here?

Danny Mum said.

/

Darren Danny, Elias, Elias, Danny.

Danny We live next door to each other Darren.

/

Darren Come on let's go then. I'll think about what you said.

Elias *is back in the kitchen. He looks at the marks on the table, turns to pick up a box, and then leaves.*

Scene Eighteen: into Family together III

Maggie *has just arrived from London.*

She has stopped in a nearby town to collect an Indian takeaway, which she is holding in a white plastic bag.

She stands at the entrance to the farm kitchen where now, there is hardly anything left – apart from the odd moving box. The house is nearly empty.

However, the kitchen table and chairs remain.

Maggie *takes off her coat, as per the year before. This time* **Bonnie** *isn't here.*

Maggie *walks around the kitchen, without her sister, perhaps for the first time in thirty years.*

Maggie *puts on Joni Mitchell's 'Big Yellow Taxi' on the record player and looks again at the kitchen.*

Hannah *enters.*

Hannah Yes.

Maggie Hey!

Hannah I've missed you so much. Don't it always seem to go!

Maggie Put up a parking lot!

Hannah I can smell curry.

Maggie Thought I'd bring something for you all.

Alina *and* **Elias** *enter.*

Hannah It's been non-stop, mum, honestly.

Alina Almost done. **Alina** *and* **Maggie** *embrace.*

Act Two: EASTER 2026, Scene Eighteen 57

Maggie I just can't imagine how hard it's been. I'm here for a few days, so if there's anything that I can do . . .

Elias We sold some things on Facebook Marketplace today.

Peter *enters.*

Peter Alright.

Maggie Hi

Peter No call — in advance?

Maggie I'm just up for the weekend.

Peter Right.

Maggie Anyway, let's eat.

/

So lovely to see you all.

So, how's it all been going? What's new Alina?

Alina Well, I've submitted my thesis.

Maggie Well, that is brilliant isn't it.

Alina I'm very proud of it.

/

Maggie What about you, Peter?

Peter Do you guys remember Ed Godwin?

Hannah Yeah.

Peter Well, he called me after the funeral. And offered me a job.

Hannah Oh. Well, that's amazing. In Glastonbury, right?

Peter They've got a massive head of cattle. And they need another herdsman. So —

Hannah — So, you're off.

Peter We're off! (*Referring to* **Alina**) Comes with a cottage, bills paid.

Alina I've been offered a post-doc in Bristol.

Maggie That's amazing. I'm so pleased for you.

Peter You know, it just makes sense.

Alina But we don't start until September, so before all that we're going to Ukraine.

Hannah What?

Alina I wanted Peter to meet the family.

Peter Hello, my name is Peter [*in Ukrainian*]

Alina My mother will meet us in the west. It's pretty safe there now.

Hannah Oh guys, that's amazing.

Alina Just for the week. But yeah . . .

Peter It'll be nice.

Maggie Wow, so it's all change here. Full steam ahead.

Peter And I know Ed really well, and he's confident I'll pick up the job quickly. So yeah.

Peter *goes to get the annual general meeting file.*

One last time?

Maggie Is there any point? I mean, seriously.

Peter I just wanted you to see some of the final figures, who gets what, what's still outstanding.

Maggie Oh no, that's okay, I'm not expecting anything.

Peter No, but I think you'll be surprised, actually. There's more. We've sold a couple of things ahead of the farm sale to a couple of local boys and we actually got more than we were anticipating.

Act Two: EASTER 2026, Scene Eighteen 59

And with everything that's going to auction, the estimates are good, according to the auctioneer.

Lots of interest in the rest of the equipment, lots of interest in the flock. So, yeah, if anyone's up for a trip to the auction tomorrow, I'm going to be there. Watching it unfold.

What about you Han? What's the future hold?

Hannah Erm. Well I dunno. Different sorts of options presenting themselves at the moment.

Peter Oh right, like what, promotions?

Maggie That sounds very mysterious!

Hannah It does, doesn't it.

Peter So not even your mother doesn't know!

Maggie Oh, I'm always the last to know. Which is right and proper.

Hannah It's all very recent.

Peter Abroad?

Hannah It's kind of the opposite of abroad.

Maggie Oh my god stop being so bloody mysterious, spit it out.

Hannah I don't really know how to say it. The Americans, Rachel and Bartlett, I think they've offered me a job.

Alina Here?

Peter You think?

Hannah Yeah, they've offered me a job.

Maggie Amazing. What sort of job?

Hannah Estate manager.

Peter Estate manager? We never had one of those, did we?

Elias Here?

Hannah Yep.

Alina And you will do it?

Peter Estate manager.

Hannah I don't know yet, I'm just sort of telling you guys, I've literally just been asked.

Peter What are you going to manage on a farm with nothing?

Hannah Vineyards.

Peter Vineyards? Oh right, OK.

Maggie Where are they putting vineyards?

Hannah I don't know yet. But they've got some really interesting / plans.

Peter What do you know about vineyards?

Maggie Peter let her talk, and then you'll probably find out about it.

Peter Sorry sorry sorry. I'm overstepping. Estate manager. Nice ring to it.

Hannah It would be good for the soil.

Alina I think vineyards are interesting.

Peter Paying you well?

Hannah Well obviously this is not going down well is it.

/

Maggie I think it's great, and Alina seems to think it's entirely appropriate.

Peter What do you think is great about it?

Maggie Well, why not? No one's got a monopoly on what Hannah decides to do with her life.

Hannah Mum, mum, thanks, but — You've got a right to be upset Peter, but don't you think it might potentially be good to have a member of the family on the farm, so I can help steer things in the right direction.

Peter You think they'll listen to you?

Hannah Maybe.

Peter You *do* think they'll listen to you.

Maggie Peter, you've sorted out your part of things, so live and let live.

Peter Aunty Maggie is right. Aunty Maggie strikes again. Did you bring pudding Maggie or? Or just the amazing takeaway.

Hannah Peter, I didn't actually need to bring this up. I brought it up out of respect, and potentially getting your blessing, which was a mistake. Elias?

Peter *leaves.* **Maggie** *leaves.*

Elias Whatever makes you happy. Hannah.

Hannah Yeah, I know. What about you?

Elias I don't know Hannah.

Elias *leaves.*

Hannah Elias, wait. Ellas. Fuck sake. This fucking family!

Things settle. After a moment of clearing up, **Hannah** *continues.*

Sorry.

Alina It's okay. Do what you have to do.

Hannah I'm really happy for you both. Will you tell him I love him?

Alina He knows. Hannah what you're trying to do here, it's really important.

Alina *leaves without* **Hannah** *seeing.*

Hannah I was kind of hoping that you'd — fuck.

Hannah *is now alone in the farm kitchen.*

She takes a deep breath and pours a glass of wine.

She takes hold of the AGM file and starts reading.

She is sitting in **Bonnie**'s *chair.*

Scene Nineteen: Maggie, Bartlett and Hannah

Hannah *is asleep with the AGM folder.*

Bartlett *comes in with his metal detector and a bottle of kombucha as gifts.* **Bartlett** *doesn't quite realise* **Hannah** *is asleep.*

Bartlett Hannah. Hi.

Hannah Oh. What's this?

Bartlettt This is a gift from mom. It aids digestion. And this is a Viking 1. This was my first. I thought you'd like to be my partner-in-crime.

Hannah That's a beautiful gift. I got you this.

Hannah *hands* **Bartlett** *a map.*

Bartlett Ah, a map of Wells-next-the-Sea. For when 5G fails us. You must be exhausted? Emotionally speaking.

Hannah I am, yes. Thank you. But I'm happy to get going.

Bartlett You are?

Hannah Yes. Please. Sit. I've looked over your plans already. And I've added in my thoughts. The smokehouse, here, and the vineyards, they're starting here and going all the way up here, into the orchard.

Bartlett That's right.

Act Two: EASTER 2026, Scene Nineteen   63

Hannah Right. We'll come back to that. And I was thinking — thank you for offering the windmill.

Bartlett Mi casa es su casa.

Hannah But maybe we could use the windmill as a sort of base camp for the teaching farm?

Bartlett Like Everest?

Hannah Sure.

Maggie *enters.*

Maggie Oh, I'm so sorry to interrupt.

Hannah This is Maggie, my mum.

Maggie I'm just leaving. Sorry to interrupt.

Bartlett Not at all. It is a complete honour. Third-generation.

Maggie Yes.

Bartlett You two do look alike.

/

Bartlett Do you know what, I'm desperate for the little boy's room.

Bartlett *exits.*

Maggie So. This is it.

Hannah Yeah, are you ok?

Maggie I'm just happy for you.

Hannah Are you actually? I just wanted to talk to you. Well, tell you before everyone else.

Maggie Are you ok?

Hannah I am. Is there anything. Anything you need before you leave?

Bartlett *re-enters.*

Bartlett No towel. No towel.

Maggie Do you know what I did. I did actually want to check Bartlett that you have taken into account, taken into account with your plans, the wild plum tree, the big one, next to the barn.

Bartlett Which barn?

Maggie This one. It's in blossom at the moment. It's a white blossom with coral-coloured stamens.

Bartlett Oh right —

Maggie — Yeah so that tree has a preservation order on it.

Bartlett Ok.

Maggie Yeah, so that means you can't just cut it down I'm afraid.

Bartlett Ok.

Maggie Also, that's where we've put Bonnie's ashes.

/

Bartlett Maybe we could put a plaque there or —

Maggie No. No, I don't want a plaque. That tree is what's called indigenous.

No-one planted it. It sowed itself. And it needs another, just like it, in order to produce fruit. And there are some others going into the orchard. So where are you putting this vineyard? Sorry, do you mind me asking?

Barlett Well, we went with our own . . .

Hannah Agronomist.

Bartlett Ron was, you know. The vineyard is going to be a lot bigger than we originally thought. We had no idea how perfect infertile soil was going to be —

Maggie — So you are going to plant over the orchard? That's such a shame, actually.

Hannah Mum.

Bartlett Just because of the soil.

Maggie No because the roots run deep with fruit trees. That's the whole point. It doesn't matter what happens to the climate, they will always find water.

Bartlett Hands up. Do you know what. This is where my knowledge – never underestimate / the power of local / knowledge . . . falls short

Maggie / Yes it first fruited when me and Bonnie were little.

Bartlett You're absolutely right but for decades Ron has been incorrectly advising you.

Maggie Hannah knows. Hannah ought to know what I'm talking about.

/

Bartlett You know we're trying our best. I haven't asked Peter yet, but his flock could graze between the vines.

Hannah He's selling the flock at auction tomorrow. They've already left the farm.

Bartlett Oh. Too bad. Look, the most important thing is that we respect —

Maggie — No it's not just about respect. It's about the story of the land.

Hannah Mum you're preaching to the converted, here.

Maggie I don't know if I am.

Bartlett Well said.

/

Maggie Can you. Can you both just give me a moment please. In this kitchen. On my own before I leave. I think I just want a moment.

Bartlett Of course.

Bartlett *leaves.*

Hannah Yes. No problem mum. Take your time.

Hannah *leaves.*

Maggie *sits at the farm table. She looks at the toy tractor. She places her hands on the table. She puts her head on the table as she did with* **Bonnie** *that one last time.*

Maggie *is saying goodbye.*

Scene Twenty: Peter and Darren at livestock auction

A series of lambing gates come into the kitchen, setting up a livestock auction.

The sounds of sheep in pens.

The lights of an livestock auction appear.

Danny *and* **Elias** *come to sit at the farm table.*

Maggie *leaves the farm table.*

Peter *appears at the auction, with a polystyrene cup of tea. He looks at the livestock lots. The flock of sheep appear.*

Danny *and* **Elias** *lay out toy sheep on the table.*

We hear the sound of the auctioneer.

Darren *unexpectedly appears on the straw bales.*

Peter *sees* **Darren. Darren** *doesn't see him.*

Bidding for the sheep begins.

Darren *keeps bidding, gradually buying up all of* **Peter**'s *flock.*

Peter *leaves dejected.*

Scene Twenty One: Danny, Elias, Darren and Peter

Darren *makes his way down the straw bales towards the kitchen.*

He sees **Danny** *and* **Elias**, *holding hands at the kitchen table.*

Danny *and* **Elias** *are looking at* **Elias**'s *toys from when he was a boy.*

The sound of the auction fades away.

Danny   And these were all yours?

Elias   Yeah, when we were kids. Dad bought us these. And wait . . . *(taking out more)* these and these. A whole farm on our kitchen table. I think dad used to plan the next year, working, whilst playing with us.

Danny   I wish I could remember your dad.

Darren *jumps down and into the kitchen.*

Elias   Darren. What are you doing in here?

Elias *is up and away from the table.*

Danny *joins him.*

Darren   Carry on. Don't let me disturb you. Sit down. Why you being weird? You're obviously having a lovely little chat. Crack on. I'll be as silent as a lamb.

They don't carry on.

Darren *raises his voice.*

Elias   We were talking just about erm . . . when my dad got us these little toy sheep.

Darren   In character Elias. I said carry on, don't talk to me. Little sheep, your dad. Fascinating.

Elias   I think dad used to plan the next year, working, whilst playing with us actually.

Darren   Actually, why don't you shut up.

Elias How did you get in here Darren?

Darren I'm feeling very changeable today. Didn't expect to see you here Danny. Or maybe I did. Got your little lambs in front of you. Play. Time. Seems like you've been doing quite a lot play time.

Elias I don't feel comfortable with you being in here Darren.

Darren Sit down. I just bought some sheep. At the auction.

Elias You bought Peter's sheep?

Darren Yeah, Inspector Clouseau.

/

Elias I'm just going to outside for some air —

Darren No, you sit down. I'd like to talk to you two fuckers.

Peter *enters*.

Darren Oh, here we go. Oh, it's a proper party now. Thanks for inviting me into your kitchen.

Peter What is this?

Darren I don't know. I don't know yet.

Peter You're confused. You're lost.

Darren Speak up, I can't here you.

Peter Listen, Darren.

Darren WHY IS EVERYONE BEING SO TENTATIVE. FUCKING SPEAK UP.

Peter So much aggression Darren.

Darren Say what you see Peter? Say what you see.

/

Peter I see a lost boy who's on his own.

Act Two: EASTER 2026, Scene Twenty One

Darren *pours himself a cup of cold tea from the pot and sits at the table.*

Darren See, I think. And this is just a little theory that I've got.

Peter Go on.

Darren Is that lost boy might be you. I've got my sheep, I've got my farm, own two legs and I've got god.

Peter You're confused.

Darren Really weak people talk about other people.

Peter *takes a seat close to* **Darren.**

/

Peter Darren — you need to be very careful being in here. This isn't your house. You are trespassing. You've lost a lot in your life.

Darren My life? What about yours, ey.

Peter Yeah. I've lost stuff.

Darren Oh, you've lost your mum haven't you.

Peter Yeah. We've lost stuff. But we had a connection with our mum. We had a bond. Unlike your mu —

Darren — Oh, shall I pull up a sofa! Shall I have a lie down. Ladies and gentlemen, I give you Peter Carter, the psychoanalyst.

The mistake you make Peter, is that you think that I'm fucking stupid.

Peter You burnt down our barns Darren. You went in prison for it. You're going back if you make one more false move.

Darren Are you threatening me, because it sounds like you might be? WHERE DO WE GO NOW?

70   Black Sheep

Peter   You go home. You go next door —

Darren   Oh, shit I do have to go actually. Fuck. I've got to kill some sheep haven't I? Leave them to rot on your driveway. Oh, hang on, I forgot, not your driveway anymore, is it?

To **Elias** *and* **Danny.**

Good luck, you two.

And Peter. Whatever it is you think. We own our farm. We are proper farmers. You're a shadow of yourself boi, and you'll be forgotten by the next harvest.

Darren *leaves.*

'For God so loved the fucking world.'

Peter *waits. He looks at* **Elias.**

Peter *clears up the tea.*

Peter *picks up a piece of flint and begins to sharpen his knife at the kitchen table. Sparks fly across the table.*

Peter *puts the flint and knife down, and slowly leaves.*

Elias *and* **Danny** *slowly pick up the toy tractors, sheep and other farm objects, symbolising the Carters leaving the farm.*

They leave together.

Scene Twenty Two: Bartlett begins to realise

One year on.

Bartlett *is at the top of the windmill trying to speak to* **Rachel**.

Bartlett   I know mom, yes I tried that. I've been trying for a year. The district council said no. And I think here 'no,' means no.

Are you coming back this Easter . . . Ok sure. I understand I've got a lot on too . . . It's going well . . .

Act Two: EASTER 2026, Scene Twenty Two

No I don't know how many pots have been sold, I'll get Hannah to email the sales figures.

Good news, the vines are in . . . eight years mom — you wanted sparkling.

You know, mom I never envisaged this. This was your idea to re-trace our family steps.

Rachel *hangs up on him.*

Bartlett *begins to talk to the audience.*

I got smitten, I have to admit, these big Norfolk skies. Hannah was my rock at the start. But she got headhunted, dream job. She went with my blessing.

Three years later, we were making good progress, the vines had taken to the soil and the footfall to the gallery had increased. That hadn't stopped me from being the butt of the joke at the Horseshoes.

2029 — The rains came and they just didn't stop for nearly 6 months. Floods well past the flint wall, eventually they receded late summer. But the saltwater had done their damage to the soil and to the vines.

2030 — I'm feeling very alone in the farmhouse. The climate is hotter and wetter.

2031 — I see Hannah, on the quay at Blakeney. She's a mom now. She shares with me about being a farmer in England — and I suppose being a farmer anywhere — she said it took her eighteen years before she was accepted. And I thought to myself, I'm not going to wait until 2049 for a nod of acceptance.

Raf planes fly over **Bartlett***, and he leaves forever.*

Act Three: EASTER 2049

Scene Twenty Three

Plastic dust sheets fly down over the kitchen, covering it.

The years tick by.

Under the dust sheets, we see the Carters and Hendersons together again.

Gradually, the family leave one by one.

The lights are dim, showing the farm kitchen holding time over many years following the departure of the Carters and Hendersons.

The slow passing of time of the flint walls and original floor, beams and windows.

As we approach 2049, the light begins to re-appear, like a new dawn.

*We see **Sandra**, an estate agent, standing in the kitchen.*

***Sandra** should be played by the same actor who plays **Bonnie** and **Heather**.*

She looks around the kitchen with a sad smile.

She prepares herself to meet potential purchasers.

***Julie** and **Sam**, members of the Blakeney Housing Association enter.*

Sandra Hi, hello. I'm Sandy.

Julie I'm Julie, this is Sam.

Sandra You found it ok?

Sam Yep — we're only based on Blakeney island.

Sandra Ah yes, Blakeney Housing Association. Your story really is an inspiration.

Act Three: EASTER 2049, Scene Twenty Three

Sam Thank you. 103 years and still going strong.

Julie So, we know the site well – I remember when this was stables.

Sam And I remember when it was the Americans.

Sandra Now that is a long time ago.

/

Julie Most of our members have all stayed in the area. They all have a birth-tie. Demand is through the roof since the 'Right to Stay' bill was passed under the coalition.

Sam We're looking to build around thirty stilted flint and clay brick cottages across the site.

You know, using the same materials as the old Cley cottages.

Sandra Well, that's amazing.

Well, there's power running to those buildings from when it was a winery. As for freshwater, saltwater incursion in the aquifer is a bit of an issue. But the neighbouring farm has a rainwater capture system. And there's a covenant that they share with all land in a five mile radius. Still owned by the Dixons. Elias and Danny Dixon - their daughter, Bea, just took over and is really friendly. Works in animal welfare.

Then of course there's this house.

Sam Yes, we think we'd like to try and save this house and the out buildings. Hard engineer some sort of sea wall around it. There could be community spaces. There are some positive moves for that in the association.

Sandra Well — I certainly think the wider North Norfolk community will get behind the bid.

Julie I think we need to go back to our members, check what everyone's best and final could be.

Sam I don't suppose you know what the final sold prior figure is, by any chance?

Sandra I'm afraid not, we're not strictly meant to share that. But it sounds like such a brilliant project. Thanks Sam. Thanks Julie.

Sandra *is left alone. She looks through her file again, preparing for the arrival of* **Rex** *and* **Adrian** *from the National Trust.*

Sandra Hi! Rex and . . .

Adrian Adrian.

Sandra Adrian. Hello. So, have you've had a good look around? You're primarily focused on the buildings, is that right?

Rex Yes, and the National Trust feels that the landscape meets the criteria, so we're very positive about this.

Adrian — And to be able to walk around a former Norfolk farm will be so interesting for our members.

Rex Adrian, the gift shop we think could be in the old lambing shed.

Sandra Yes, lots of original features here. Well — if the National Trust wanted to think about a base here to showcase farming, then this could be a great fit, yes. I'm afraid, the lambing shed is now listed, but I can see a visitor centre or a UX room in the windmill. That's where the great view of the sea is, where the old marsh used to be. Absolutely gorgeous.

Adrian Rex, if we could lose the lambing shed, it'd be perfect for charging points.

Rex And Sandra, there's been an attempt at trying to bring this out of brownfield status before, is that right?

Sandra Yes, there's been a few attempts. You probably know this was fully agricultural land from the 1930s. But — typical story — it was overfarmed in the late twentieth-century, so arable wasn't really viable anymore.

Rex Farmers know best!

Act Three: EASTER 2049, Scene Twenty Three

Adrian *laughs.*

Sandra Then there was livestock, a vineyard — but I think the degraded soil was just too big a hurdle in the end. So, what we're seeing now is just nature slowly coming back.

Adrian It's so sad, isn't it? When our heritage is systematically worn away.

Sandra I suppose it depends on what you mean by heritage really.

Rex I heard Blakeney HA have shown an interest. If anyone's proposing to develop this site, we'd really like to talk to them. The National Trust and King George VII is really interested in investing in Norfolk again, as a dedication to his late father Wiilliam and after the closure of Sandringham.

Sandra Sure, sure. It's my job to keep everyone as informed as possible.

Rex And the reserve price is, what, about 6 million Euro, give or take.

Sandra I'm not really allowed to say, but I think that would be competitive.

Adrian We'll be in touch.

Sandra Great.

Sandra *is left alone. She looks through her file again, preparing for the arrival of* **Petra**.

Sandra Hello, I'm Sandy. Welcome.

Petra Petra.

Sandra Petra, of course. You're my four o'clock. Have you come far?

Petra (*in Ukranian*) I'm based in Paris. But I have family in the West Country.

Sandra Sorry I just needed. So, you have come far! I gather you have plans to bring farming back to Oyster Catcher?

Sandra puts in her translation device.

Petra Yes, that's right — but not quite like the old days.

Sandra You are aware that this is now designated brownfield?

Petra I think I can work with that.

Sandra What sort of farming are you interested in?

Petra Vertical farming. So that's basically indoors.

Sandra Well, the farm has passed through quite a few hands in the last decade and most of them have added buildings — that could be helpful for you?

Petra Do they have three-phase power?

Sandra Not in the south fields, but there's been a brewery, a vineyard, even a little museum at one point in most of the sheds around the courtyard so they should be linked up.

The lambing shed is listed, I'm afraid, but otherwise you can do what you like.

Petra I'd like to keep the exteriors as they are.

Sandra Is it just you?

Petra Used to be eleven of us in my company. But we're a small team now. Most of my processes are automated so it'd just be me and my family living here.

Sandra Brilliant. So, you could run the farm remotely at times. Avoid the baking hot Norfolk summers.

Petra Yes.

/

Sandy, the farmhouse. Does it come with any furniture?

Act Three: EASTER 2049, Scene Twenty Three

Sandra A lot of it has been stripped, the previous owners were just using the house for storage. But the Aga is still there — they go on forever. Oh, actually I noticed this big old table in the barn that looks as though it's been here since the Second World War.

It was a family home for nearly 100 years, and I think you can feel that, can't you?

/

Petra This is where my parents met.

Sandra No. Really? Did they know the Carters?

Petra My father was a Carter. My mother came here as a student from Ukraine.

Sandra Who was your father?

Petra Peter Carter.

Sandra No! I remember Peter — we were at primary school together! He was a total rascal. I can see it now; you're Peter Carter's daughter.

Peter *appears on the straw bales.*

The sounds of the Norfolk wildlife can be heard in the distance.

/

Sandra So, it's not just about the business. It's . . . I want that connection to him.

Sandra *can see* **Petra** *looking around taking in the warmth of the kitchen.*

Sandra Listen Petra. Look, I'm going to write a number down on here.

Sandra *has found the original AGM file under a sheet of plastic.*

Now this may, or may not be the sold prior figure, and you might not want to have a sneaky look at that whilst I'm out in the old farmyard.

I'll just be outside. By that old plum tree. You can take your time.

Sandra *leaves.*

Petra *goes to take a look at the figure. She smiles. She looks up and around at the kitchen.*

She takes **Peter**'s *chair at the kitchen table.*

She looks under the dust sheet and begins to pull it away.

She reveals the pile of soil on the table. The music swells.

She puts her hands on the table. Really feels the table.

She puts her hand in the soil. She smells the soil.

Generations of farming in the palm of her hand.

She smells again.

The music soars.

The lights fade.

This farm is safe, for generations to come.

Discover. Read. Listen. Watch.

A NEW WAY TO ENGAGE WITH PLAYS

This award-winning digital library features over 3,000 playtexts, 400 audio plays, 300 hours of video and 360 scholarly books.

Playtexts published by Methuen Drama, The Arden Shakespeare, Faber & Faber, Playwrights Canada Press, Aurora Metro Books and Nick Hern Books.

Audio Plays from L.A. Theatre Works featuring classic and modern works from the oeuvres of leading American playwrights.

Video collections including films of live performances from the RSC, The Globe and The National Theatre, as well as acting masterclasses and BBC feature films and documentaries.

FIND OUT MORE:
www.dramaonlinelibrary.com • @dramaonlinelib

Methuen Drama Modern Plays

include

Bola Agbaje	Barrie Keeffe
Edward Albee	Jasmine Lee-Jones
Ayad Akhtar	Anders Lustgarten
Jean Anouilh	Duncan Macmillan
John Arden	David Mamet
Peter Barnes	Patrick Marber
Sebastian Barry	Martin McDonagh
Clare Barron	Arthur Miller
Alistair Beaton	Alistair McDowall
Brendan Behan	Tom Murphy
Edward Bond	Phyllis Nagy
William Boyd	Anthony Neilson
Bertolt Brecht	Peter Nichols
Howard Brenton	Ben Okri
Amelia Bullmore	Joe Orton
Anthony Burgess	Vinay Patel
Leo Butler	Joe Penhall
Jim Cartwright	Luigi Pirandello
Lolita Chakrabarti	Stephen Poliakoff
Caryl Churchill	Lucy Prebble
Lucinda Coxon	Peter Quilter
Tim Crouch	Mark Ravenhill
Shelagh Delaney	Philip Ridley
Ishy Din	Willy Russell
Claire Dowie	Jackie Sibblies Drury
David Edgar	Sam Shepard
David Eldridge	Martin Sherman
Dario Fo	Chris Shinn
Michael Frayn	Wole Soyinka
John Godber	Simon Stephens
James Graham	Kae Tempest
David Greig	Anne Washburn
John Guare	Laura Wade
Lauren Gunderson	Theatre Workshop
Peter Handke	Timberlake Wertenbaker
David Harrower	Roy Williams
Jonathan Harvey	Snoo Wilson
Robert Holman	Frances Ya-Chu Cowhig
David Ireland	Benjamin Zephaniah
Sarah Kane	

Methuen Drama Contemporary Dramatists

include

John Arden (two volumes)
Arden & D'Arcy
Peter Barnes (three volumes)
Sebastian Barry
Mike Bartlett
Clare Barron
Brad Birch
Dermot Bolger
Edward Bond (ten volumes)
Howard Brenton (two volumes)
Leo Butler (two volumes)
Richard Cameron
Jim Cartwright
Caryl Churchill (two volumes)
Complicite
Sarah Daniels (two volumes)
Nick Darke
David Edgar (three volumes)
David Eldridge (two volumes)
Ben Elton
Per Olov Enquist
Dario Fo (two volumes)
Michael Frayn (four volumes)
John Godber (four volumes)
Paul Godfrey
James Graham (two volumes)
David Greig
John Guare
Lee Hall (two volumes)
Katori Hall
Peter Handke
Jonathan Harvey (two volumes)
Iain Heggie
Israel Horovitz
Declan Hughes
Terry Johnson (three volumes)
Sarah Kane
Barrie Keeffe
Bernard-Marie Koltès (two volumes)
Franz Xaver Kroetz
Kwame Kwei-Armah
David Lan
Bryony Lavery
Deborah Levy
Doug Lucie
Alistair MacDowall
Sabrina Mahfouz
David Mamet (six volumes)
Patrick Marber
Martin McDonagh
Duncan McLean
David Mercer (two volumes)
Anthony Minghella (two volumes)
Rory Mullarkey
Tom Murphy (six volumes)
Phyllis Nagy
Anthony Neilson (three volumes)
Peter Nichol (two volumes)
Philip Osment
Gary Owen
Louise Page
Stewart Parker (two volumes)
Joe Penhall (two volumes)
Stephen Poliakoff (three volumes)
David Rabe (two volumes)
Mark Ravenhill (three volumes)
Christina Reid
Philip Ridley (two volumes)
Willy Russell
Eric-Emmanuel Schmitt
Ntozake Shange
Sam Shepard (two volumes)
Martin Sherman (two volumes)
Christopher Shinn (two volumes)
Joshua Sobel
Wole Soyinka (two volumes)
Simon Stephens (five volumes)
Shelagh Stephenson
David Storey (three volumes)
C. P. Taylor
Sue Townsend
Judy Upton (two volumes)
Michel Vinaver (two volumes)
Arnold Wesker (two volumes)
Peter Whelan
Michael Wilcox
Roy Williams (four volumes)
David Williamson
Snoo Wilson (two volumes)
David Wood (two volumes)
Victoria Wood

For a complete listing of
Methuen Drama titles, visit:
www.bloomsbury.com/drama

Follow us on Twitter and keep up to date
with our news and publications
@MethuenDrama